ŠEVČÍK

VIOLIN STUDIES

OPUS 1 PART 3

SCHOOL OF VIOLIN TECHNIQUE

SCHULE DER VIOLINTECHNIK

MÉTHODE DE LA TECHNIQUE DU VIOLON

BOSWORTH

BOE005048
ISMN: M2016 4068 6
Music settting by Musonix

Cover design: Miranda Harvey
Cover picture: The Farmouth Stradivari, Cremona 1692 (Antonio Stradivari)
© Christie's Images Ltd. 2000

Exclusive Distributors:
Hal Leonard
7777 West Bluemound Road
Milwaukee, WI 53213
Email: info@halleonard.com

Hal Leonard Europe Limited
42 Wigmore Street
Marylebone, London, W1U 2RN
Email: info@halleonardeurope.com

Hal Leonard Australia Pty. Ltd.
4 Lentara Court
Cheltenham, Victoria, 3192 Australia
Email: info@halleonard.com.au

OTAKAR ŠEVČÍK OPUS 1

Seit ihrem Erscheinen im Jahr 1901 bildeten die Werke Ševčíks auf der ganzen Welt die Grundlage vieler unterschiedlicher Streicherschulen. Tausende von Spielern schätzen Ševčík nach wie vor als durch nichts zu ersetzende Hilfe bei der instrumentaltechnischen Ausbildung.

Bei der Erarbeitung von Ševčík stehen wie beim Skalenspiel, bei Etüden oder bei eigentlichen Werken immer vier Teilbereiche im Mittelpunkt der Aufmerksamkeit: die Reinheit der Intonation, die Reinheit und Gleichmäßigkeit der Tongebung, rhythmische Genauigkeit und schließlich die rein technische Souveränität und Leichtigkeit. Im folgenden sind einige technische Aspekte genannt, die es bei der Erarbeitung von Op. 1 zu beachten gilt:

Linker Daumen. Der linke Daumen sollte leicht am Hals der Geige aufliegen. Übt der Daumen einen stärkeren Druck aus, wächst entsprechend auch der Fingerdruck und umgekehrt. Der Spieler sollte sich immer darum bemühen, Druck der Finger und Gegendruck des Daumens möglichst gering zu halten.

Zwischen dem Daumen und dem Grundgelenk des ersten Fingers sollte etwas Platz bleiben. Ungeachtet der normalen Position des Daumens ist es beim Einüben der Fingerbewegungen oft hilfreich, den Daumen weit vorzuziehen, zwischen den ersten und zweiten Finger oder dem zweiten Finger gegenüber. Auf diese Weise wird der Daumen daran gehindert, einen starken Gegendruck oder einen seitlichen Druck gegen das Grundgelenk des ersten Fingers auszuüben.

Bewegung der Finger. Die Finger bewegen sich mit der größten Leichtigkeit, wenn die Hauptbewegung aus dem Grundgelenk heraus erfolgt, bewegungsmäßig völlig unabhängig von der Hand. Die Hauptbewegung sollte keinesfalls durch Öffnen oder Schließen des mittleren Fingergelenks ausgelöst werden. Die Stellung der Finger bleibt weitgehend gleich, ganz egal, ob sie sich gerade auf oder über der Saite befinden.

Wo immer möglich, sollten die Fingerspitzen über den Saiten bleiben. Im langsamen Tempo kann man die Finger etwas höher anheben, so dass sie deutlich artikulierend auf die Saite herabfallen können. Im schnellen Tempo müssen die Finger dicht an den Saiten bleiben. Sobald ein Ton gegriffen wurde, sollte die Fingerspannung nachlassen. Die Hand wird fest, wenn die Finger nach dem Bewegungsschema „greifen-drücken" und nicht nach dem Schema „greifen-loslassen" agieren.

Der Ellbogen unterstützt die Aktivität der Finger durch eine leichte Positionsverlagerung je nach gerade gespielter Saite. Spielt man auf der G-Saite, wendet sich der Ellbogen etwas mehr zur E-Saite; spielt man auf der E-Saite, wiederum etwas mehr zur G-Saite. Übungen, die nur auf einer Saite notiert sind (wie beispielsweise die Nr. 1 nur auf der A-Saite), sollten auch auf den anderen Saiten geübt werden, wobei Ellbogen und Hand entsprechend angepaßt werden müssen.

Welcher Teil der Fingerspitze? Der genaue Aufsetzpunkt der Fingerspitze oder Kuppe hat Auswirkungen auf die Handstellung, diese wiederum auf das Handgelenk und die Haltung des linken Armes. Wenn der Finger zu sehr an der linken Spitze aufgesetzt wird (die zur Schnecke zeigende Seite) dann können die Finger sich leicht zu sehr zum ersten Finger hinwenden und aneinander kleben. Wenn der Finger andererseits zu stark mit dem rechten Teil der Kuppe aufgesetzt wird (die dem Steg zugewandten Seite), kann es passieren, dass die Finger zum Steg hin wegkippen.

Vibrato. Die Übungen von Ševčík sollten mit und ohne Vibrato geübt werden. Dabei ist das Vibrato klein zu halten, um die Intonation nicht zu beeinträchtigen. Beim Üben sollte man sich um ein kontinuierliches Vibrato bemühen. Ziel ist es, das Vibrato von einem Finger zum nächsten weiterfließen und nicht mit jedem neuen Finger erneut ansetzen und enden zu lassen.

Dynamik und Bogenführung. Die Fingerbewegungen sollten in jeder Lautstärke von p bis f geübt werden. Der Fingerdruck in der linken Hand muss auch dann gering bleiben, wenn der Bogen starken Druck auf die Saite ausübt. Der Fingerdruck links sollte für einen reinen Ton gerade ausreichend, dabei aber so gering als möglich sein.

Der Spieler sollte sich bewusst um die Einhaltung des besten Kontaktpunkts zwischen Bogen und Saite bemühen, also weder zu nah am Steg noch zu nah am Griffbrett streichen.

Köpfchen statt Muskeln. Ohne einen Befehl vom Kopf können sich unsere Finger nicht bewegen. Daher ist das Spielen der Ševčík-Übungen genauso sehr Kopftrainig wie Fingertraining. Die Klarheit der geistigen Vorstellung dessen, was wir spielen wollen, ist eines der wichtigsten Elemente, um den richtigen Einsatz der Finger vorzubereiten. Dies wird wesentlich einfacher gelingen, wenn man ein Stück musikalisch und inhaltlich verstanden hat; einfacher als es nur mechanisch einzustudieren. Höre aufmerksam in die Musik hinein, die du machst, dann kannst du Tongebung und Klang so lange durch Fingerhaltung und Bogenstrich verbessern, bis das Stück deinen Vorstellungen entspricht.

Fortschritte aufzeichnen. Markiere die Übungen, Takte oder Abschnitte, die du schon gemacht hast. Dies heißt nicht, dass du die markierten Passagen schon perfekt beherrschst, sondern lediglich, dass du die Übung in Angriff genommen hast. Du kannst sie bei passender Gelegenheit wiederholen und erneut markieren. Auf diese Weise kannst du dir die Reihenfolge der Übungen selbst auswählen, je nach den Anforderungen der Stücke, die du gerade übst oderwas dich gerade besonders interessiert. Auch vermeidest du durch die Kennzeichnung, Übungen zu oft zu wiederholen und andere zu vernachlässigen. Häufig ist es sinnvoller, bestimmte Übungen über verschiedene Tage zu wiederholen, anstatt ständig neues Übungsmaterial zu probieren. Das einfache Wiederholen vertieft die Übungen und lässt sie ruhig, leicht und selbstverständlich gelingen.

SIMON FISCHER
London, 2000
Übersetzung: D. Goebel und D. Fratz

OTAKAR ŠEVČÍK   OPUS 1

Since they first appeared in 1901, Otakar Ševčík's works have formed the basis of many schools of string playing around the world. Thousands of players continue to find Ševčík an invaluable aid to technical development.

In practising Ševčík, as in playing scales, études or pieces, there are always four main headings to consider: purity of intonation, purity and evenness of tone, exactness of rhythm, and physical freedom and ease. A few specific technical points to watch out for in Opus 1 are as follows:

Left thumb. Rest the thumb lightly against the neck of the violin. The more the thumb presses, the more the fingers press, and *vice versa.* Always aim for minimum finger pressure, minimum thumb counter-pressure. Keep an open space between the thumb and the base joint of the first finger. Whatever your normal thumb position, when practising the finger patterns it is often helpful to keep the thumb well forward, between the first and second fingers or opposite the second. This ensures that the thumb cannot squeeze tightly back, or sideways, against the first-finger base joint.

Finger action. The fingers move with the greatest freedom when the main movement is from the base knuckle joint, moving completely independently of the hand. The primary movement is never an opening or closing at the middle joint of the finger. The shape of the fingers when on the string, or above the string, should remain basically the same.

Wherever possible keep the tips of the fingers above the strings. At slow speeds the fingers may be raised slightly higher so that they drop with greater articulation. At fast speeds keep the fingers close to the strings. There should be an immediate release as soon as a finger stops a note on the string. The hand tightens if the finger action is 'stop-press' rather than 'stop-release'. The elbow helps the fingers by taking a slightly different position for each string. It is positioned a little more towards the E string when playing on the G string, a little more towards the G string when playing on the E string. When the exercises are written on one string (e.g. No. 1 is written only for the A string), practise those patterns on the other strings as well, adjusting the elbow and hand accordingly.

Which part of the fingertip? The exact part of the fingertip or pad which is in contact with the string affects the angle of the hand, and this in turn affects the wrist and the position of the left arm. If there is too much of the left side of the fingertip (the side nearest to the nut) on the string, the fingers may lean over too much towards the first finger, and also squash together. Too much of the right side of the fingertip on the string (the side nearest the bridge) may cause the fingers to collapse over towards the bridge.

Vibrato. Practise Ševčík finger patterns with and without vibrato. Keep the vibrato minimal so that it does not distort the intonation. Practise continuity of vibrato, so that the vibrato does not start and stop with each individual finger, but rather flows from one finger into the next.

Dynamics and bowing. Practise the finger patterns at all dynamics from *p* to *f.* When the bow plays heavily into the string make sure that the left-hand finger pressure remains light, i.e. as much finger pressure as necessary (for a pure tone), but as little as possible. Take care to maintain the best point of contact: bow neither too near to the bridge nor too near to the fingerboard.

Mind, not muscles. The fingers cannot move without a signal from the brain, so practising Ševčík is as much a matter of training the mind as of training the muscles. The clarity of the mental picture is the single most important element in gaining real control of the fingers. This is made much easier if you approach the exercises musically and artistically, rather than purely mechanically. Listening carefully, so that you catch every single sound that comes out of the instrument, strive to make the finger patterns sound both beautiful and expressive.

Keeping track. Mark with a tick every bar, line or section you work on. A tick does not have to mean that the section is 'perfect', only that you have practised it. You can always practise it again on other occasions, giving it another tick each time. Keeping a record in this way means that you can play the exercises in any order you like, and can go directly to whatever seems particularly relevant or interesting at the time; and you always know what you have already played, so that you can gradually work through the entire volume without repeating some sections whilst neglecting others. It is often best to concentrate on the same section over several days, rather than using completely new material in each practice session. Simple repetition then engrains the patterns so that they become smooth, effortless and automatic.

SIMON FISCHER
London, 2000

OTAKAR ŠEVČÍK   OPUS 1

Dès leur première parution en 1901, les ouvrages d'Otakar Ševčík ont constitué le support d'innombrables écoles de violon à travers le monde. Des milliers d'interprètes continuent à y trouver un outil inestimable pour l'approfondissement de la technique violonistique.

En travaillant Ševčík, de même qu'en jouant gammes, études ou morceaux, quatre principes fondamentaux sont toujours à considérer: la pureté de l'intonation, la pureté et l'égalité de la sonorité, l'exactitude rythmique, l'indépendance et l'aisance physiques. On s'attachera, dans l'Opus 1, aux quelques spécificités techniques suivantes:

Pouce gauche. Appuyez avec légèreté le pouce contre le manche du violon. Plus le pouce fait pression, plus la pression des doigts augmente et vice versa. Recherchez toujours le plus petite pression des doigts et la plus petite contre-pression du pouce.

Maintenez un espace ouvert entre le pouce et l'articulation inférieure de l'index. Quelle que soit la position normale de votre pouce, il est souvent utile, lors du travail des doigtés, de garder le pouce bien en avant, entre l'index et le médium ou face au médium. Ceci évite que le pouce n'appuie trop fort en arrière, ou de côté, sur l'articulation inférieure de l'index.

Agilité des doigts. Les doigts se déplacent avec plus d'agilité quand le mouvement principal provient de l'articulation de la première phalange, dans une action complètement indépendante de la main. Le principe du mouvement consiste à ne jamais ouvrir ou fermer le doigt à l'aide de son articulation médiane. La courbure des doigts sur la corde, ou au-dessus de la corde, doit rester fondamentalement la même.

Quand cela est possible, maintenez le bout des doigts au-dessus des cordes. Dans les mouvements lents, on peut légèrement relever les doigts de façon à ce qu'ils retombent avec un plus grande articulation. Dans les mouvements rapides, gardez les doigts proches des cordes. La pression d'une note sur la corde doit être immédiatement suivie d'une détente. La main se raidit si l'action du doigt est celle de 'pression-tension' plutôt que 'pression-détente'.

Le coude renforce les doigts en prenant une position légèrement différente pour chaque corde. Il se place un peu plus vers la corde de *mi* quand on joue sur la corde de sol, un peu plus vers la corde de *sol* quand on joue sur la corde de *mi*. Lorsque les exercices sont écrits pour une seule corde (le No. 1, par exemple, n'utilise que la corde de la), travaillez ces formules aussi sur les autres cordes en replaçant convenablement le coude et la main.

Quelle partie du bout des doigts? La partie précise du bout ou du gras du doigt en contact avec la corde affecte l'angle de la main et, donc, le poignet et la position du bras gauche. Si l'on pose le bout du doigt trop sur son côté gauche (vers le sillet de la touche) sur la corde, les doigts, trop penchés vers l'index, auront tendance à se serrer les uns sur les autres. Si l'on le pose trop sur son côté droit (vers le chevalet), les doigts risquent de s'affaisser vers le chevalet.

Vibrato. Travaillez les formules de doigtés de Sevčík avec et sans *vibrato*. Maintenez le vibrato à son niveau minimal afin de ne pas fausser l'intonation. Entraînez-vous à la continuité du vibrato de façon à ce qu'il ne commence ni ne s'arrête à chaque changement de doigt mais coule sans interruption d'un doigt à l'autre.

Nuances dynamiques et coups d'archet. Travaillez les formules de doigtés sur toutes les nuances du *p* au *f*. Lorsque l'archet frotte lourdement sur la corde, assurez-vous que la pression des doigts de la main gauche demeure légère, c'est-à-dire suffisante mais aussi réduite que possible. Appliquez-vous à maintenir le meilleur point de contact, ni trop près du chevalet, ni trop près de la touche.

L'esprit, pas les muscles. Les doigts ne pouvant se mouvoir sans un signal provenant du cerveau, travailler les exercices de Ševčík revient donc à exercer autant l'esprit que les muscles. La clarté de l'image mentale demeure le principe unique et essentiel permettant l'acquisition d'une réelle maîtrise des doigts. Celle-ci est facilitée par une approche plus musicale et artistique que purement mécanique des exercices. L'écoute attentive de tous les sons produits par l'instrument favorise une interprétation expressive des formules de doigtés et une belle qualité de son.

Garder des traces. Marquez d'une croix chaque mesure, chaque ligne ou chaque section que vous travaillez. Ceci ne signifie pas nécessairement que vous jouez 'parfaitement' le passage, mais simplement que vous l'avez travaillé. Vous pourrez toujours le reprendre en le marquant à chaque fois. Cette façon de procéder vous permettra d'aborder les exercices dans l'ordre que vous souhaitez et d'exercer directement les points qui vous paraissent les plus nécessaires ou intéressants à un moment donné tout en situant à tout instant ce que vous avez déjà vu. Vous étudierez ainsi l'intégralité du volume en évitant d'en répéter certaines sections et d'en négliger d'autres. Il est souvent plus profitable de se concentrer sur une section pendant plusieurs jours que de changer d'exercices à chaque séance de travail. La répétition familiarise avec les séquences de doigtés et leur exécution devient lisse, aisée et automatique.

SIMON FISCHER
London, 2000
Traduction: Agnès Ausseur

Otakar Ševčík   Opus 1

Gli studi per violino di Otakar Ševčík furono inizialmente pubblicati nel 1901 e fin da allora hanno formato la base di molte scuole di suonatori di violino nel mondo. Migliaia di musicisti continuano a considerare Ševčík un aiuto inestimabile per lo sviluppo tecnico.

Quando alle prese con gli esercizi di Ševčík, come per esempio quando si suonano delle scale, degli studi o dei brani, bisogna sempre tener presente questi quattro fattori: purezza di intonazione, purezza e consistenza di tonalità, esattezza di ritmo, scioltezza e facilità fisica. Si elencano qui di seguito alcuni specifici punti tecnici che meritano dovuta attenzione nell'Opus 1:

Pollice sinistro. Appoggiare il pollice leggermente contro il manico del violino. Più viene effettuata pressione col pollice, più aumenta la pressione delle dita, e viceversa. Bisogna sempre cercare di fare la minima pressione con le dita, onde mantenere la minima pressione col pollice. Tenere uno spazio ampio tra il pollice e la giuntura di base dell'indice. Qualunque sia la posizione normalmente adottata dal pollice, quando si studiano questi esercizi per le dita, è spesso utile avere il pollice piuttosto in avanti, tra l'indice e il dito medio, oppure di fronte al dito medio. Questo assicura che il pollice non stringa forte indietro o di lato, contro la giuntura di base dell'indice.

Il movimento delle dita. Le dita si muovono con la massima libertà d'azione quando il movimento principale proviene dalla giuntura di base del dito, cioè muovendosi con completa indipendenza dalla mano. Il movimento primario non consiste mai in un'apertura o chiusura della giuntura media del dito. L'aspetto delle dita, quano sono appoggiate sulle corde o sospese sopra le corde, dovrebbe essere sostanzialmente lo stesso.

Dove possibile, mantenere sempre le punte delle dita posate sulle corde. Nei tempi lenti le dita possono essere sollevate leggermente più in alto in modo da cadere sulla corda con maggiore articolazione. Nei tempi rapidi tenere le dita vicino alle corde. Dovrebbe sentirsi un immediato senso di allentamento non appena un dito finisce di suonare una nota sulla corda. La mano tende a serrarsi se l'azione delle dita è 'blocca-premi' invece di 'blocca-libera'. Il gomito aiuta le dita nell'assumere una posizione leggermente diversa per ciascuna corda; è in posizione più diretta verso la corda del *Mi* quando viene suonata la corda del Sol ed è un pò più verso la corda del *Sol* quando viene suonata la corda del *Mi*. Quando gli esercizi sono scritti soltanto su una corda (per esempio il N. 1 è scritto solo sulla corda del *La*), studiare sulle altre corde con i medesimi esercizi, correggendo dunque la posizione del gomito e della mano.

Quale parte della punta delle dita? L'esatta parte della punta delle dita o del polpastrello che viene a contatto con la corda influisce sull'angolazione della mano, e questo a sua volta influisce sul polso e la posizione del braccio sinistro. Se si usa troppo il lato sinistro del polpastrello (quello più vicino alla nocetta) sulla corda, le dita potrebbero pendere troppo verso l'indice e magari stringersi insieme. L'impiego eccessivo della parte destra del polpastrello sulla corda (il lato più vicino al ponticello) può causare il crollo delle dita verso il ponticello.

Vibrato. Studiare gli esercizi per le dita con e senza vibrato. Mantenere il vibrato al minimo in modo da non distorcere l'intonazione. Studiare il vibrato con continuità in modo che abbia un'inizio ed una fine con ogni dito individuale e che possa scorrere senza interruzione tra un dito e l'altro.

Le dinamiche e i colpi d'arco. Studiare gli esercizi per le dita in tutte le dinamiche da *p* a *f*. Quando l'arco suona in modo pesante sulla corda, bisogna stare attenti a che le dita della mano sinistra rimangano lievi, cioè che premano il meno possibile ma quanto sia necessario per ottenere un'intonazione pura.

Prestare attenzione nel mantenere il migliore punto di contatto, cioè di non appoggiare l'arco troppo vicino al ponticello o o troppo vicino alla tastiera.

La mente, non i muscoli. Le dita non sono in grado di muoversi senza prima aver ricevuto il segnale dal cervello, perciò nello studiare Ševčík è ugualmente importante allenare sia la mente che i muscoli. La chiarezza dell'immagine mentale è l'unico elemento ed il più importante nella conquista del vero controllo delle dita. Questo è reso più facile se si affrontano gli esercizi in maniera musicale e artistica piuttosto che in modo puramente meccanico. Ascoltando con attenzione, in modo da cogliere ogni singolo suono che emana dallo strumento, durante lo studio degli esercizi si faccia ogni sforzo per ricavarne suoni che siano insieme belli ed espressivi.

Annotazioni. Spuntare ogni battuta, riga o parte studiata. Questo segno non significa necessariamente che tale parte sia 'perfetta' ma semplicemente che l'avete studiata. Potete sempre studiarla di nuovo in altre occasioni, marcando l'esercizio ogni volta. Tenendo queste annotazioni, vuol dire che si possono studiare gli esercizi in qualsiasi ordine si voglia, mirando direttamente all'esercizio che sia relevante o particolarmente interessante in quel momento; in questo modo siete sempre al corrente di ciò che avate già suonato, finchè riuscirete gradualmente a studiare tutto il volume senza il pericolo di ripetere alcune parti e tralasciarne altre. Spesso è meglio concentrarsi sulla stessa parte per diversi giorni, invece di usare del materiale completamente nuovo ogni volta che si studia. La semplice ripetizione fa sì che gli esercizi diventino ben consolidati in modo da diventare sciolti, agevoli ed automatici.

SIMON FISCHER
London, 2000
Traduzione: Anna Maggio

Vorwort des Herausgebers

Die Neuausgabe eines Werkes, das auf seinem Gebiet einen „Klassiker" darstellt, darf man nicht auf die leichte Schulter nehmen. Ein Technik-Handbuch vom Rang der Ševčík Violinstudien stellt dabei eine große Herausforderung dar. Der Herausgeber sieht sich dabei nicht nur einer völlig anderen, neuen Generation gegenüber. Auch die Verantwortung gegenüber aktuellen Entwicklungen und Strömungen ist in Einklang zu bringen mit dem Erhalt der wichtigen Eigenheiten des Werkes; es kommt auf eine gute Balance zwischen Erneuern und Erhalten an!

Die Originalausgabe erschien anfang der 20er Jahre. Sie trägt inzwischen deutliche Spuren ihres Alters sowohl im äußeren Erscheinungsbild von Notenstich und Seitenbild als auch in der Wortwahl. Dass das Werk bis heute überdauert hat, beweist die Schlüssigkeit des großen Rahmens, in dem das Werk konzipiert ist. Mein Ziel war als, seine attraktiven und bestens erprobten Bestandteile und Grundzüge zu erhalten und Abhilfe zu schaffen, wo der Originaltext über die Jahre mehr oder weniger ungebräuchlich geworden ist.

Die meisten deutschen Abkürzungen sind beibehalten worden. Trotzdem sind einige wenige Termini ausgemustert worden im Interesse einer einheitlichen Stilistik der Bände untereinander.

Die sorgfältigen Übersetzungen der Originalausgabe zu Artikulation und Bogentechnik waren nicht immer glücklich. Es wurde versucht, aus dem Deutschen heraus mit beinahe wörtlichen Übersetzungen ins Englische, Französische, Italienische, Tschechische und Russische die Ševčík'schen formulierungen herüberzuretten. (Kurioserweise sind italienische Standardbegriffe, wie z.B. *staccato*, aus dem deutschen Text mit einem anderen Wort ins Italienische zurückübertragen worden.) Dies führt nicht nur zu konstruiert wirkenden Formulierungen, es irritiert auch sachlich. So wurde in dem Bemühen, die Texte möglichst authentisch zu Übertragen bisweilen genau das Gegenteil erreicht, indem der Wort-für-Wort-Übersetzung der Vorzug vor einer sinnechten Übersetzung gegeben wurde.

Um hier eine klare Linie zu ziehen, wurde auf internationale Standardausdrücke zurückgegriffen. So muss z.B. *spiccato* ohne die deutsche Übersetzung „geworfen" auskommen, auch die italienische Übersetzung „sciolto balzato" ist nicht gebräuchlich und also entfernt worden; *jeté* ist nicht übersetzt zu „werfend", „thrown", „jerked", „balzato" oder „di rimbalzo"; *saltando* steht auch für die überflüssigen Übersetzungen „springend", „hopping", „sautillé", „saltellato" und „saltato"; *volante* für „fliegend", „flying", „volant"; *martellato* für „gehämmert", „hammered", „martelé"; und *staccato* für „gestoßen", „chopped" oder „picchettato (secco)". (Unglücklicherweise verwirrt die alte Ausgabe hier auch noch mit dem Begriff „detaché".) Ohne Zweifel lässt diese Liste die — unbeabsichtigten — feinen Bedeutungsunterschiede erkennen zwischen den gebräuchlichen Fachbegriffen und den hölzernen Übersetzungen.

Letztlich befleißigt sich die Ausgabe einer modernisierten Notenschrift und eines ansprechenden, zeitgemäßen Layouts, womit eine bessere Lesbarkeit der Ševčík-Übungen erreicht wird, so dass man die Studien einfach lieber in Angriff nimmt. Einige offensichtliche Fehler wurden beseitigt und die Übungsanweisungen gestrafft und sprachlich aktualisiert.

MILLAN SACHANIA
Shepperton, England, 2000
Übersetzung: D. Fratz

EDITORIAL PREFACE

Preparing a new edition of a work which is a classic in its field is a task that cannot be lightly undertaken. A manual of technique as prestigious as the Ševčík Violin Studies presents its own challenges. In renovating it, the editor must not only consider new and potential users of the work; there is also a responsibility to relieve existing, experienced users of needless fuss and discomfort in 'up-grading' to the new edition. This calls for a balanced approach, one which blends innovation with conservation.

The previous edition first appeared in print at the beginning of the twentieth century. It showed signs of its age both in its notational style and in the quality of the engraving and image. Yet its durability attested to the strength of its broader conception. My aim has thus been to retain its most attractive and well-established features whilst remedying those defects which detracted from its usefulness. Accordingly, most of the German abbreviations of the former edition have been retained. A few, however, have been jettisoned in the interests of stylistic consistency between the volumes.

In its quest for linguistic parity, the former edition painstakingly translated much of the terminology denoting bowing styles and articulation. Generally starting from the German, it supplied equivalents in English, French, Italian, Czech, and Russian. (Curiously, though, the older edition often reserved standard Italian terms such as 'staccato' for the directions in the languages *other* than Italian; in these cases, the Italian directions deployed an alternative Italian word or phrase.) This practice served not only to clutter the text, but also to confuse. For though the intention was almost certainly to provide the closest equivalent in the language concerned (borne out by the consistency of the 'translations'), inevitably the translations sometimes carried different nuances of meaning from those suggested by the original concepts. In the interests of clarity, the present edition uses standard international terminology. *Spiccato* appears without the attendant German 'geworfen' and the alternative Italian 'sciolto balzato'; *jeté*, without the attendant 'werfend', 'thrown', 'jerked', 'balzato', 'di rimbalzo'; *saltando* is given in place of 'springend', 'hopping', 'sautillé', 'saltellato', 'saltato'; *volante* for 'fliegend', 'flying', 'volant'; *martellato* for 'gehämmert', 'hammered', 'martelé'; and *staccato* for 'abgestoßen', 'chopped', and 'picchettato (secco)'. (Incidentally, the previous edition sometimes confused 'détaché' with 'staccato'.) Doubtless the preceding list will be valuable to users who none the less wish to note the subtle distinctions between the standard terms used in the present edition and the attendant 'translations' found in the previous edition — distinctions which were almost certainly not intended.

Finally, the new edition modernises the notational practice; this, together with the more generous layout, has much increased the legibility of Ševčík's exercises. Patent errors have been corrected, and all the written instructions have been re-drafted so that they may better reflect modern idiom in the languages represented.

MILLAN SACHANIA
Shepperton, England, 2000

PRÉFACE DE L'ÉDITEUR

Etablir une nouvelle édition d'une oeuvre qui est un classique dans son domaine est une tâche qu'on ne peut entreprendre à la légère. Un traité de technique aussi prestigieux que les études pour violon de Ševčík présente des défis particuliers. En le révisant, l'éditeur ne doit pas seulement considérer ses nouveaux utilisateurs potentiels, il lui revient également de ne causer ni embarras, ni inconfort inutiles à ses utilisateurs fidèles et expérimentés par son actualisation. Ceci suppose une approche équilibrée qui mêle innovation et tradition.

L'édition précédente, imprimée pour la première fois au début du vingtième siècle, manifestait des signes de vieillissement tant par son style de notation que par la qualité de sa gravure et de son graphisme. Néanmoins, sa longévité témoignait de la force de sa largeur de conception. Mon objectif a donc été d'en retenir les traits les plus attractifs et reconnus tout en corrigeant les défauts qui compromettaient son efficacité. En conséquence, la plupart des abréviations allemandes de l'édition précédente a été retenue. Quelques-unes ont toutefois été abandonnées au profit de la cohérence stylistique entre les volumes.

Dans sa quête de parité linguistique, l'ancienne édition donnait une traduction laborieuse à partir, généralement, de l'allemand vers l'anglais, le français, l'italien, le tchèque et le russe de nombreux termes définissant les styles de coups d'archet et de phrasé. (Assez curieusement, les termes italiens conventionnels tels que 'staccato' étaient maintenus dans les langues *autres* que l'italien, et remplacés par un autre mot italien ou une autre phrase dans les indications en italien.) Cette pratique non seulement encombrait le texte mais créait la confusion. En dépit de leur volonté certaine

(confirmée par leur homogénéité) de fournir l'équivalent le plus proche dans chaque langue, ces 'traductions' comportaient parfois, et inévitablement, des nuances de sens différentes de celles présentes dans le concept original. Pour plus de clarté, notre édition recourt à la terminologie internationale conventionnelle. *Spiccato* figure sans l'équivalent allemand 'geworfen' ni le terme italien de 'sciolto balzato'; *jeté* sans les équivalents 'werfend', 'thrown', 'jerked', 'balzato', 'di rimbalzo'; *saltando* remplace 'springend', 'hopping', 'sautillé', 'saltellato', 'saltato'; *volante* remplace 'fliegend', 'flying', 'volant'; *martellato* remplace 'gehämmert', 'hammered', 'martelé'; et *staccato* remplace 'abgestoßen', 'chopped' et 'picchettato (secco)'. (L'ancienne édition confond par ailleurs parfois 'détaché' et 'staccato'.) La liste ci-dessus sera sans doute précieuse aux utilisateurs qui souhaiteraient néanmoins s'attacher aux distinctions subtiles existant entre les termes conventionnels utilisés dans cette édition et les 'traductions' équivalentes rencontrées dans l'ancienne édition — distinctions qui n'avaient presque sûrement rien d'intentionnel.

Enfin, la notation de la nouvelle édition a été modernisée, ce qui, associé à une mise en page plus aérée, a beaucoup amélioré la lisibilité des exercices de Ševčík. Les erreurs évidentes ont été corrigées et toutes les indications écrites ont été re-rédigées de façon à refléter la forme actuelle des langues représentées.

MILLAN SACHANIA
Shepperton, Angleterre, 2000
Traduction: Agnès Ausseur

PREFAZIONE DELL'EDITORE

La preparazione di una nuova edizione di un'opera diventata oramai un classico nel suo campo, è un lavoro che non si puó intraprendere alla leggera. Un manuale di tecniche cosí prestigioso quanto quello per gli Studi del Violino di Ševčík puó presentare certe sue difficoltà. Nell'apportare le nuove modifiche, l'editore deve considerare non solo i nuovi e potenziali utenti dell'opera; esiste inoltre una responsabilità verso coloro che già sono a conoscenza degli esercizi, onde alleviare loro da qualsiasi difficoltà e rendere agevole la 'transizione' dalla vecchia alla nuova edizione. Questo richiede un approccio che sia equilibrato, cioè una revisione che unisca innovazione a conservatismo.

L'edizione precedente uscì per la prima volta in stampa agli inizi del ventesimo secolo. Tale edizione mostra segni di un'epoca passata, sia per lo stile della notazione musicale, che per la qualità di stampa ed immagine. Nonostante questo, la sua durabilità costituisce una testimonianza della solidità di una più ampia concezione. Il mio obbiettivo è stato quindi quello di ritenere le caratteristiche interessanti consolidate, eliminando quei difetti che ne riducevano la loro praticità. In conseguenza, la maggior parte delle abbreviazioni in tedesco sono state mantenute. Alcune, comunque, sono state eliminate nell'interesse di una consistenza stilistica tra i vari volumi.

Cercando di mantenere una parità linguistica, l'edizione precedente minuziosamente traduceva la maggior parte della terminologia denotando lo stile dei vari modi di esecuzione e articolazione. Generalmente, a incominciare col tedesco, venivano fornite le versioni equivalenti in inglese, francese, italiano, cecoslavacco e russo. (Stranamente però la vecchia edizione manteneva spesso termini standard in italiano quali 'staccato' nelle istruzioni date nella lingua *non* italiana; in questi casi le istruzioni date in italiano disponevano di una frase o di una parola alternativa.) Questa pratica servì non solo a rendere il testo troppo denso, ma anche a confondere. Peciò anche se l'intenzione era quella di dare il significato più vicino alla lingua in questione (supportate dalla consistenza delle 'traduzioni'), inevitabilmente le traduzioni davano a volte diverse sfumature di significato da quelle suggerite originariamente. Per maggior chiarezza, la presente edizione usa una traduzione standard della terminologia internazionale. *Spiccato* appare senza la corrispondente tedesca 'geworfen' e l'alternativa in italiano 'sciolto balzato'; *jeté*, senza la corrispondente 'werfend', 'thrown', 'jerked', 'balzato', 'di rimbalzo'; *saltando* sostituisce 'springend', 'hopping', 'sautillé', 'saltellato', 'saltato'; *volante* per 'fliegend', 'flying', 'volant'; *martellato* per 'gehämmert', 'hammered', 'martelé'; e *staccato* per 'abgestoßen', 'chopped' e 'picchettato (secco)'. (E' da notarsi che l'edizione precedente qualche volta confondeva 'detaché' con 'staccato'.) Senza dubbio la lista che precede sarà d'aiuto a coloro che nonostante tutto vogliono osservare attentamente le distinzioni tra i termini standard usati nella presente edizione e le rispettive 'traduzioni' trovate nell'edizione precedente — distinzioni che quasi sicuramente non erano volute.

Da ultimo, la nuova edizione aggiorna la pratica di notazione; questa, unita all'aspetto più largo della stampa, ha aumentato di molto la leggibilità degli esercizi di Ševčík. Sono stati corretti errori palesi ed il testo delle istruzioni è stato nuovamente redatto per meglio riflettere l'idioma moderno della lingua rappresentata.

MILLAN SACHANIA
Shepperton, Inghilterra, 2000
Traduzione: Anna Maggio

Abkürzungen und Zeichen

G	Ganzer Bogen
H	Halber Bogen
Fr	Am Frosch des Bogens
M	Mitte des Bogens
Sp	Spitze des Bogens
Fr...Sp	Vom Frosch bis zur Spitze
Fr...M	Vom Frosch bis zur Mitte
M...Sp	Von der Mitte bis zur Spitze
1＿＿	Die Finger auf der Saite liegen lassen
⊓	Abstrich
∨	Aufstrich
–	Breit stoßen
·	*Staccato* oder *martellato*
▾	*Jeté, spiccato* oder *saltando*

Abréviations et signes

G	Tout l'archet
H	Moitié de l'archet
Fr	Du talon de l'archet
M	Du milieu de l'archet
Sp	De la pointe de l'archet
Fr...Sp	Du talon jusqu'à la pointe
Fr...M	Du talon jusqu'au milieu
M...Sp	Du milieu jusqu'à la pointe
1＿＿	Laisser les doigts en place
⊓	Tiré
∨	Poussé
–	Détaché large
·	*Staccato* ou *martellato*
▾	Jeté, *spiccato* ou *saltando*

Abbreviations and Symbols

G	Whole bow
H	Half bow
Fr	Frog-end of bow
M	Middle of bow
Sp	Tip of bow
Fr...Sp	From the frog to the tip
Fr...M	From the frog to the middle
M...Sp	From the middle to the tip
1＿＿	Hold the fingers down on the string
⊓	Down-bow
∨	Up-bow
–	Broadly detached
·	*Staccato* or *martellato*
▾	*Jeté, spiccato* or *saltando*

Abbreviazioni e Segni

G	Tutto l'arco
H	Metà dell'arco
Fr	Tallone
M	Mezzo dell'arco
Sp	Punta dell'arco
Fr...Sp	Dal tallone alla punta dell'arco
Fr...M	Dal tallone al mezzo dell'arco
M...Sp	Dal mezzo dell'arco alla punta
1＿＿	Lasciare le dita ferme
⊓	In giù
∨	In su
–	Staccato lungo
·	Staccato o martellato
▾	*Jeté,* spiccato o saltando

Opus 1

III

Otakar Ševčík
(1852–1934)

LAGENWECHSEL *	CHANGES OF POSITION *	CHANGEMENTS DES POSITIONS *	CAMBIAMENTO POSIZIONI *
Jedes Beispiel gestoßen und gebunden üben.	Practise each exercise staccato and legato.	Travailler chaque exercice détaché et lié.	Studiare ogni esercizio legato e staccato.

No. 1

Tonleitern auf einer Saite	Scales on one string	Gammes sur une corde	Scale su una corda

* Siehe Op. 1/ii, Nr. 4, 5, 16, 24, 25.   * See Op. 1/ii, Nos. 4, 5, 16, 24, 25.   * Voir Op. 1/ii, Nos. 4, 5, 16, 24, 25.   * Vedi Op. 1/ii, Ni. 4, 5, 16, 24, 25.

No. 2

| Tonleitern durch drei Oktaven | Scales over three octaves | Gammes sur trois octaves | Scale di tre ottave |

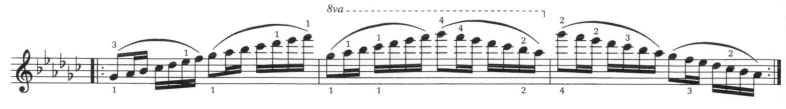

| Die Tonleitern sind auch auf folgende Arten zu üben: | Also practise the preceding scales in the following ways: | Etudier aussi les gammes des manières suivantes: | Studiare le precedenti scale anche nelle maniere seguenti: |

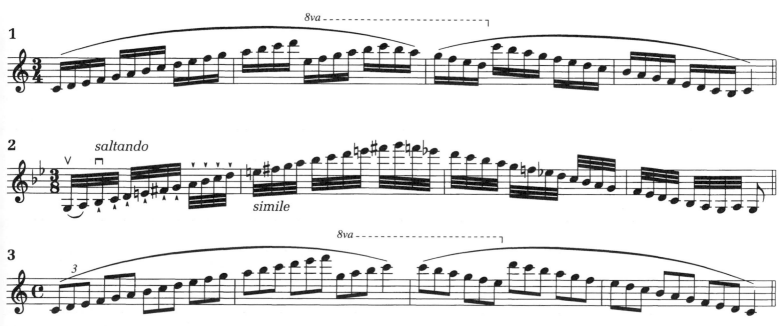

8

No. 3

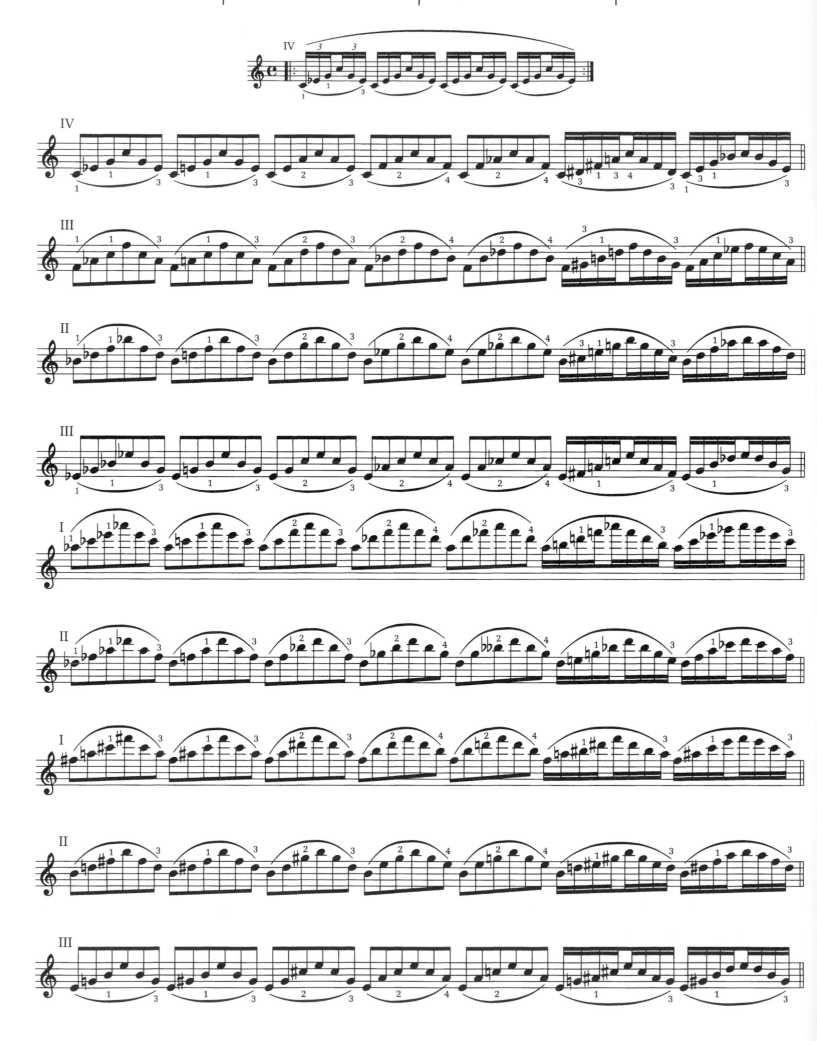

9

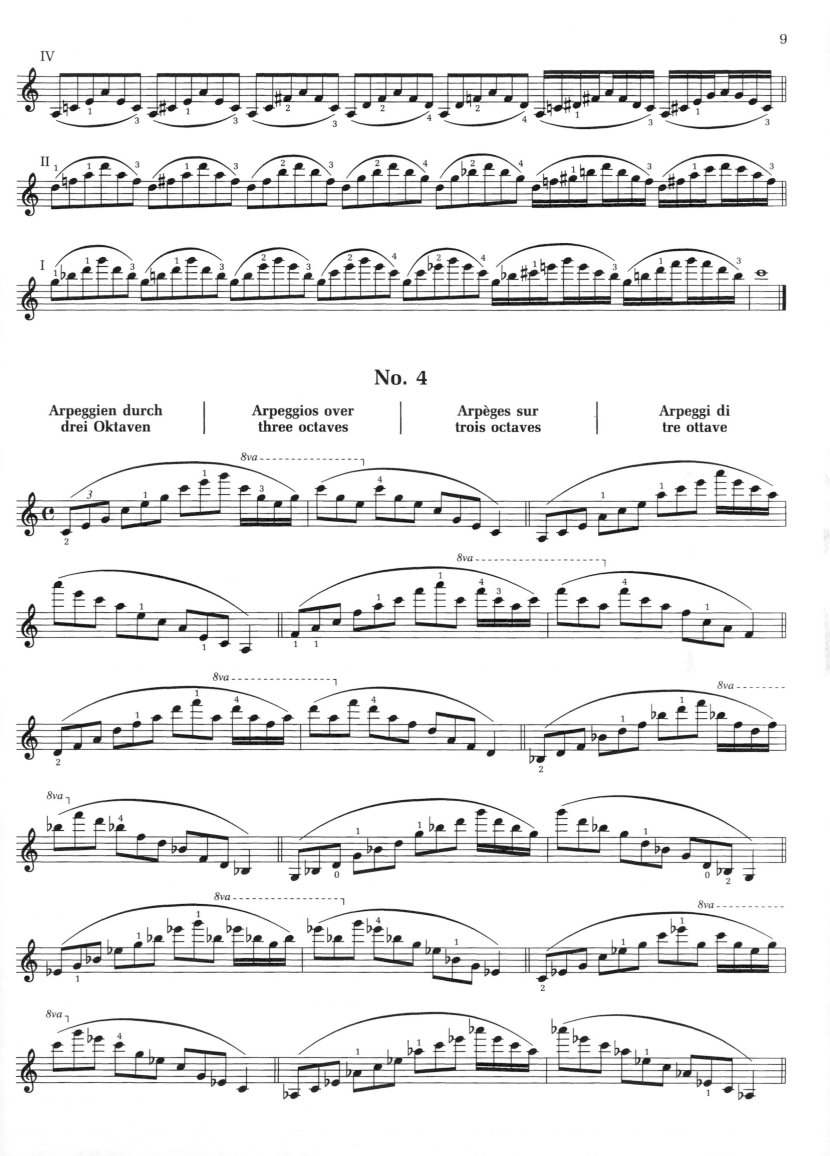

No. 4

| Arpeggien durch drei Oktaven | Arpeggios over three octaves | Arpèges sur trois octaves | Arpeggi di tre ottave |

10

No. 5

12

14

No. 6

16

No. 7

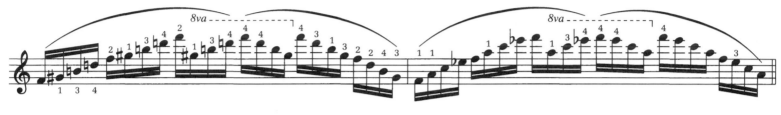

a) III

b) IV

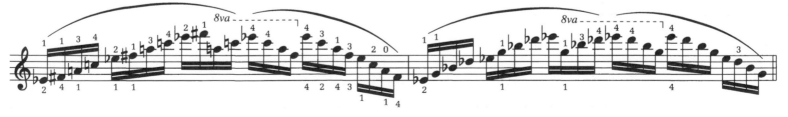

No. 8

Chromatische Tonleiter | **The chromatic scale** | **Gamme chromatique** | **Scala cromatica**

No. 9

Übungen für den Lagenwechsel	Exercises for changing position	Exercices pour le changement de position	Esercizi per il cambio di posizione

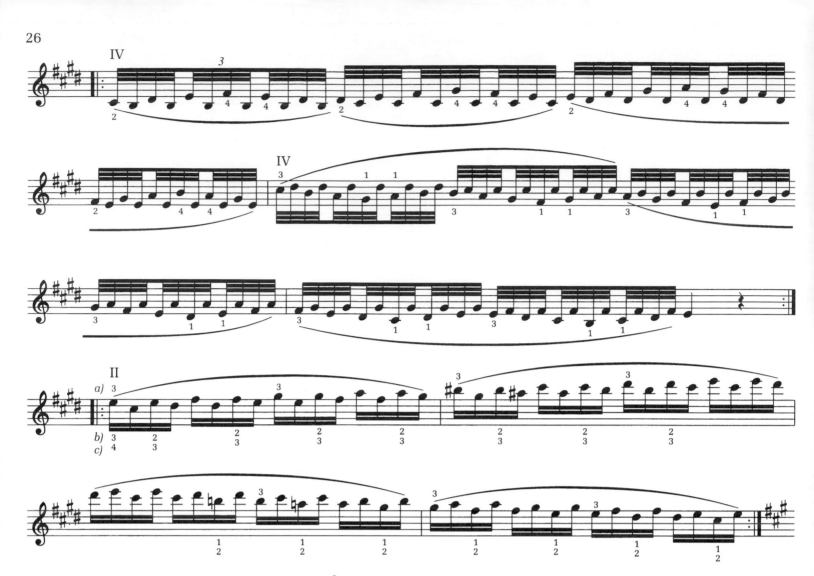

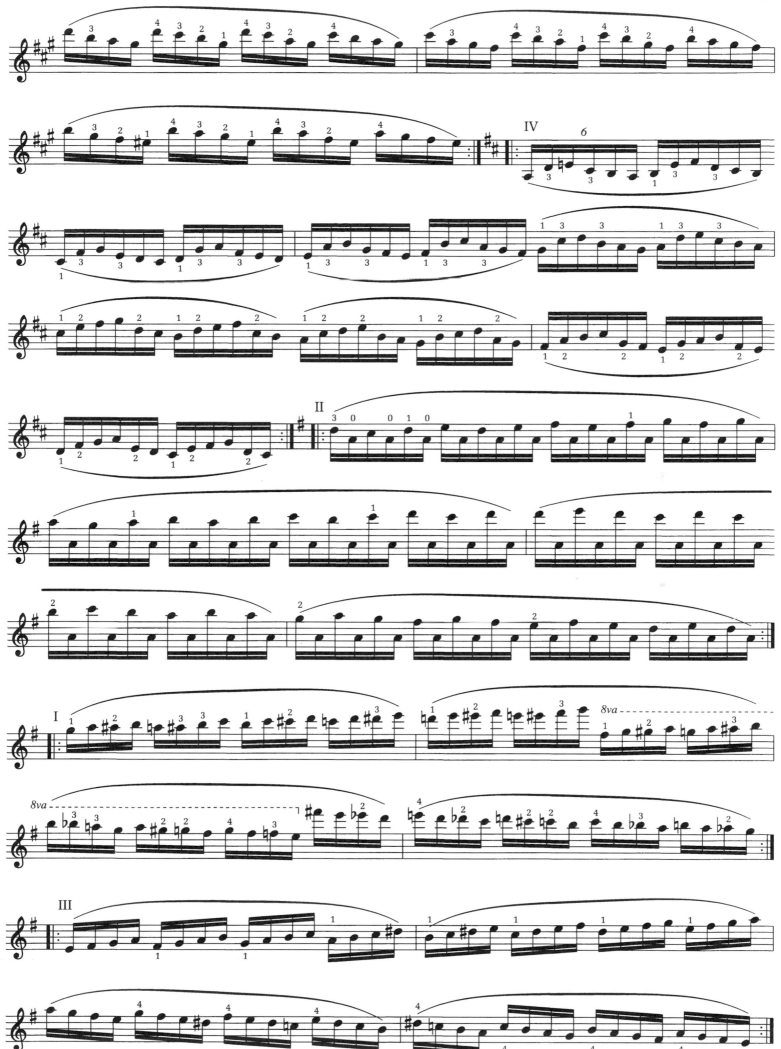

No. 10

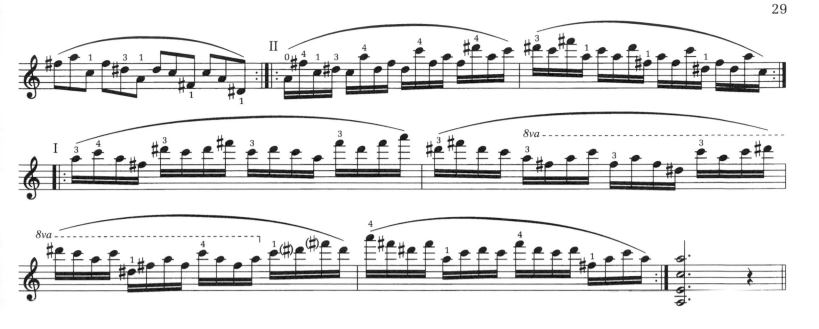

No. 11

No. 12

34

36

No. 13

Übung auf der 4. Saite	**Exercise on the 4th string**	**Exercice sur la 4e corde**	**Esercizio sopra la 4a corda**
Diese Übung ist auch auf der 1., 2. und 3. Saiten auszuführen.	Also practise this exercise on the 1st, 2nd and 3rd strings.	Exécuter cet exercice aussi sur les 1e, 2e et 3e cordes.	Studiare lo stesso esercizio anche sulla 1a, 2a e 3a corda.

No. 14

| Diese Übung ist auch auf der 2., 3. und 4. Saiten auszuführen. | Also practise this exercise on the 2nd, 3rd and 4th strings. | Exécuter cet exercice aussi sur les 2e, 3e et 4e cordes. | Studiare lo stesso esercizio anche sulla 2a, 3a e 4a corda. |

Printed and bound in Great Britain by Caligraving Limited

INHALTSVERZEICHNIS
der
SCHULE DER VIOLINTECHNIK Op. 1
von

INDEX
to the
SCHOOL OF VIOLIN TECHNIQUE Op. 1
by

SOMMAIRE
de
L'ÉCOLE DE LA TECHNIQUE DU VIOLON Op. 1
par

O. ŠEVČÍK

Zusammengestellt von
Compiled by — K. W. ROKOS
Etabli par

(Die angeführten Zahlen sind Übungsnummern, nicht Seitenzahlen)
(Figures refer to exercise numbers, not pages)
(Les chiffres indiquent le numéro de l'exercice, non celui de la page)

INHALT UND HAUPTZWECK DER ÜBUNG / CONTENTS AND MAIN AIM OF EXERCISE / NATURE ET BUT PRINCIPAL DE CHAQUE EXERCICE	OPUS 1/i — 1. Lage / 1st position / 1e position	OPUS 1/ii — 2. Lage 2nd pos.	3. Lage 3rd pos.	4. Lage 4th pos.	5. Lage 5th pos.	6. Lage 6th pos.	7. Lage 7th pos.	OPUS 1/iii — Alle Lagen / All positions / Toutes les positions	OPUS 1/iv — Doppelgriffe, Akkorde, usw. / Double-stopping, chords, etc. / Doubles cordes, cordes, etc.
Linke Finger: Geläufigkeit und Intonation / Left fingers: facility and intonation / Doigts gauches: vélocité et intonation									
Auf derselben Saite / On the same string / Sur la même corde	1, 2, 3, 4, 5, 6, 7	1, 4	12	21	30	35	39	1, 3, 9, 11	2, 3 (8^{ve}), 4 (fingered 8^{ve})
Mit Saitenwechsel / Crossing strings / Changement de cordes	10, 20	4, 5, 7	17	27	32	38	41	6, 12	2, 3, 8, 11 (6^{ths}), 12
Halbton-Verschiebungen / Semitone shifts / Changement de demi-tons	8, 9		13, 18	21, 27	32	38	41	6, 11, 12	3, 6, 9
Tonleitern (siehe auch 'Akkorde') / Scales (see also 'Chords') / Gammes (voir aussi 'Accords')	12, 19 (chrom.)	9 (chrom.)						1 (1 corda), 2 (3 oct.), 8 (chrom.)	1 (8^{ve}), 5 (3^{rds}), 10 (6^{ths}), 12 (10^{ths}), 9 (chrom.), 21 (harm.)
Gebrochene Intervalle / Broken intervals / Intervalles brisés	13 (3^{rds}), 14 (6^{ths}), 15 (8^{ve}), 16 (9^{ths} etc.)	3 (8^{ve})	15 (8^{ve})			36 (3^{rds})			6 (3^{rds})
Arpeggien / Arpeggios / Arpèges	18, 20, 21, 22	6, 8	17	23, 26	33			3, 10, 13 (1 corda), 4, 5, 7 (3 oct.)	1, 13, 14, 15, 22
Doppelgriffen / Double-stopping / Doubles cordes	17 (arp.), 23, 24, 25, 26	2 (arp.), 10	14 (arp.), 19	22 (arp.), 28	31 (arp.)	37 (arp.)	40 (arp.)		Alle Übungen / All exercises / Tous les exercices
Lagenwechsel / Changes of position / Changements de position		4, 5	16	24, 25				Alle Übungen / All exercises / Tous les exercices	2, 6, 16
Pizzicato linke Hand / Left-hand pizzicato / Pizzicato main gauche									19, 20
Triller, Verzierungen / Trills, ornaments / Trilles, ornements								9, 12	2, 3, 4, 7
Flageolettöne / Harmonics / Harmoniques								14 (nat.)	21, 22 (1 corda), 23 (2 corda)
Rechte Hand, Handgelenk, Arm / Right hand, wrist, arm / Main droite, poignet et avant-bras; Stricharten (siehe auch 'Akkorde') / Bowing variants (see also 'Chords') / Différents coups d'archet (voir aussi 'Accords')	11 (wrist / poignet / Handgelenk), 18 (arp.), 29								
Akkorde (einschl. Tonleitern, Staccato) / Chords (inc. scales, staccato) / Accords (inc. gammes, staccato)	27, 28	11	20	29	34				17, 18